Our Story

A Couple's Guided Journal To Share Their Lives, Dreams, and Hearts With Each Other

Jeffrey Mason

DEDICATION

To My Amazing Paula,

You appeared one day, and everything changed. Thank you for finding us. Your love and your belief in me has led me to become the Person I was always meant to be. The story of Us is one of trials and triumphs, dares and dreams, life and love. I Love You Paula.

IT'S YOUR BIRTHDAY!
"Take my hand and we'll make it...I swear."
— Jon Bon Jovi, *Livin' On a Prayer*

Person A

1. What is your birthdate? _____

2. What was your full name at birth?

   _____

3. Were you named after a relative or someone else of significance? If yes, who? _____

   _____

4. In what city were you born? _____

   _____

5. What was your height (length) and weight at birth?

   _____

6. Were you the oldest, middle, or youngest child? How many siblings do you have? _____

   _____

7. What were your first words? _____

   _____

IT'S YOUR BIRTHDAY!

"The greatest thing you will ever learn is to just love and be loved in return." — Nat King Cole, Nature Boy

Person B

1. What is your birthdate? _____

2. What was your full name at birth?

   _____

3. Were you named after a relative or someone else of significance? If yes, who? _____

   _____

4. In what city were you born? _____

   _____

5. What was your height (length) and weight at birth?

   _____

6. Were you the oldest, middle, or youngest child? How many siblings do you have? _____

   _____

7. What were your first words? _____

   _____

GROWING UP

"If the relationship can't survive the long term, why on earth
would it be worth my time and energy for the short term"
— Nicholas Sparks, *The Last Song*

Person A

1. Where did you grow up when you were a kid?

    _____

2. Did you have a nickname?

    _____

3. What kind of chores did you have?

    _____

4. Did you recieve an allowance? If yes, how much?

    _____

5. What was the worst trouble you remember getting

    into as a kid? _____

    _____

    _____

    _____

6. Did you have braces?

    _____

GROWING UP

"For the two of us, home isn't a place. It is a person.
And we are finally home."
— Stephanie Perkins, *Anna & the French Kiss*

Person B

1. Where did you grow up when you were a kid?

   _____

2. Did you have a nickname?

   _____

3. What kind of chores did you have?

   _____

4. Did you recieve an allowance? If yes, how much?

   _____

5. What was the worst trouble you remember getting

   into as a kid? _____

   _____

   _____

   _____

6. Did you have braces?

   _____

YOUR PARENTS

"True love is friendship set on fire."
— Molly E. Lee, *Edge of Chaos*

Person A

1. What three words would you use to describe your mother? _____

    _____

    _____

2. What three words would you use to describe your father? _____

    _____

    _____

3. Where did your parents grow up?

    _____

4. How did your parents meet? _____

    _____

    _____

5. Describe your parent's relationship.

    _____

    _____

YOUR PARENTS

"If music be the food of love, play on."
— William Shakespeare

Person B

1. What three words would you use to describe your mother? _____

   _____

   _____

2. What three words would you use to describe your father? _____

   _____

   _____

3. Where did your parents grow up?

   _____

4. How did your parents meet? _____

   _____

   _____

5. Describe your parent's relationship.

   _____

   _____

YOUR FAMILY TREE

"He is the cheese to my macaroni."
— Diablo Cody, *Juno*

Person A

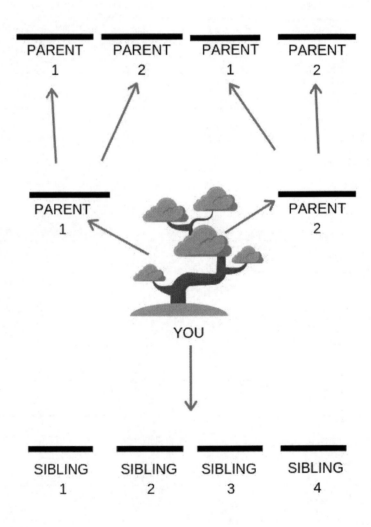

PARENT 1 PARENT 2 PARENT 1 PARENT 2

PARENT 1 PARENT 2

YOU

SIBLING 1 SIBLING 2 SIBLING 3 SIBLING 4

YOUR FAMILY TREE

"one's not half of two; two are halves of one."
– E.E. Cummings

Person B

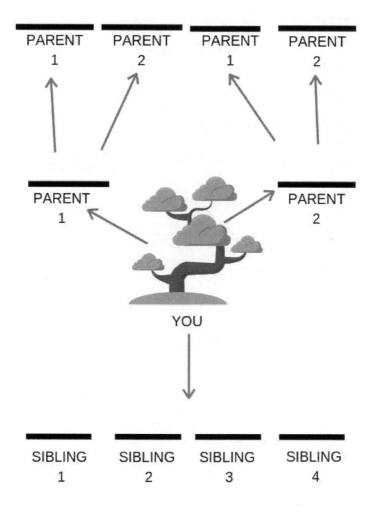

PARENT 1   PARENT 2   PARENT 1   PARENT 2

PARENT 1   PARENT 2

YOU

SIBLING 1   SIBLING 2   SIBLING 3   SIBLING 4

"I wonder
how many people
don't get
the one they want,
but end up
with the one
they're supposed
to be with."
— Fannie Flagg,
Fried Green Tomatoes

"I may not
have gone
where
I intended to go,
but I think
I have ended up
where I
needed to be."
— Douglas Adams,
*The Long Dark
Tea-Time of the Soul*

TRIVIA

"I fell in love the way you fall asleep: slowly, and then all at once." — John Green, *The Fault in Our Stars*

Person A

1. What is your favorite flavor of ice cream?

   _____

2. How do you like your coffee?

   _____

3. How do you like your eggs cooked?

   _____

4. How many speeding tickets have you received?

   _____

5. Do you still have your tonsils?

   _____

6. What is your favorite holiday?

   _____

7. What is your favorite season?

   _____

8. Do you read your horoscope?

   _____

TRIVIA

"As soon as I saw you, I knew an adventure
was going to happen." — Winnie the Pooh

Person B

1. What is your favorite flavor of ice cream?

   _____

2. How do you like your coffee?

   _____

3. How do you like your eggs cooked?

   _____

4. How many speeding tickets have you received?

   _____

5. Do you still have your tonsils?

   _____

6. What is your favorite holiday?

   _____

7. What is your favorite season?

   _____

8. Do you read your horoscope?

   _____

SCHOOL DAYS
"Never go to bed mad. Stay up and fight."
— Phyllis Diller

Person A

1. Did you enjoy school? _____

   _____

2. What were your favorite and least favorite subjects?

   _____

   _____

3. Did you participate in any school activities? What were they? _____

   _____

   _____

4. Did you play any sports? If yes, which ones?

   _____

5. In what kind of car did you learn to drive?

   _____

6. What was your hairstyle during high school?

   _____

SCHOOL DAYS

"Love is composed of a single soul inhabiting two bodies."
— Aristotle

Person B

1. Did you enjoy school? _____

    _____

2. What were your favorite and least favorite subjects?

    _____

    _____

3. Did you participate in any school activities? What
    were they? _____

    _____

    _____

4. Did you play any sports? If yes, which ones?

    _____

5. In what kind of car did you learn to drive?

    _____

6. What was your hairstyle during high school?

    _____

THE TEENAGE YEARS

"When you don't talk, there's a lot of stuff that ends up not getting said." — Catherine Gilbert Murdock, *Dairy Queen*

Person A

1. Did you go to a public or private school?

   _____

2. Did you hang out with a group of people or a small number of close friends? Are any of you still in contact? _____

   _____

   _____

3. Did you have a curfew during high school? If yes, what would happen if you were late?

   _____

4. What was a typical weekend night for you during your teens? _____

   _____

   _____

5. Did you date in high school?

   _____

THE TEENAGE YEARS

"The strongest love is the love that can demonstrate its fragility." — Paulo Coelho

Person B

1. Did you go to a public or private school?

   _____

2. Did you hang out with a group of people or a small number of close friends? Are any of you still in contact? _____

   _____

   _____

3. Did you have a curfew during high school? If yes, what would happen if you were late?

   _____

4. What was a typical weekend night for you during your teens? _____

   _____

   _____

5. Did you date in high school?

   _____

WHERE HAVE YOU LIVED?

"Anyone can live in a house, but homes are created
with patience, time and love." — Jane Green

Person A

List the cities you have lived in during your life.
Include the dates if you can remember them.

1. _____

2. _____

3. _____

4. _____

5. _____

6. _____

7. _____

8. _____

9. _____

10. _____

WHERE HAVE YOU LIVED?

"I could stay with you forever and never realize the time."
— Bob Dylan, *You're Gonna Make Me Lonesome When You Go*

Person B

List the cities you have lived in during your life.
Include the dates if you can remember them.

1. _____

2. _____

3. _____

4. _____

5. _____

6. _____

7. _____

8. _____

9. _____

10. _____

"If you
need something
from somebody
always give
that person
a way
to hand it to you."
— Sue Monk Kidd,
The Secret Life of Bees

"You don't develop
courage
by being happy
in your
relationships everyday.
You develop
it by
surviving
difficult times
and challenging
adversity."
— Epicurus

LOVE & ROMANCE
"A heart that loves is always young." — Greek Proverb

Person A

1. Who did you have your biggest crush on during your teen years? _____

   _____

2. How old were you when you had your first kiss?

   _____

3. What age were you when you had your first date? What did you do? _____

   _____

   _____

4. What is one small thing your partner can do to show you how much they care about you? _____

   _____

   _____

5. In your opinion, where is a perfect honeymoon destination? _____

6. What was the first time your heart was broken?

   _____

LOVE & ROMANCE
"Everything you can imagine is real" — Pablo Picasso

Person B

1. Who did you have your biggest crush on during your teen years? _____

   _____

2. How old were you when you had your first kiss?

   _____

3. What age were you when you had your first date? What did you do? _____

   _____

   _____

4. What is one small thing your partner can do to show you how much they care about you? _____

   _____

   _____

5. In your opinion, where is a perfect honeymoon destination? _____

6. What was the first time your heart was broken?

   _____

LOVE & ROMANCE

"True love begins when nothing is looked for in return."
— Antoine de Saint-Exupery

Person A

1. Have you ever written anyone a love poem? Have you ever received one? _____

   _____

2. What are the three most important qualities of a successful relationship? _____

   _____

   _____

3. Where were we the first time we kissed?

   _____

4. What is your idea of a perfect romantic spot?

   _____

5. What are your relationship deal breakers?

   _____

   _____

   _____

LOVE & ROMANCE

"When I count my blessings, I find you in every one."
— Richelle E. Goodrich, *Slaying Dragons*

Person B

1. Have you ever written anyone a love poem? Have you ever received one? _____

   _____

2. What are the three most important qualities of a successful relationship? _____

   _____

   _____

3. Where were we the first time we kissed?

   _____

4. What is your idea of a perfect romantic spot?

   _____

5. What are your relationship deal breakers?

   _____

   _____

   _____

HOW ROMANTIC ARE YOU?

"And remember, as it was written, to love another person is to see the face of God." — Victor Hugo, Les Misérables

Person A

1. Do you believe in love-at-first sight?

   _____

2. Do you believe in soulmates?

   _____

3. Should a proposal be a planned elaborate moment
   or quiet and intimate? _____

   _____

4. Do you save cards and letters that you are given?

   _____

   _____

5. True or False: Anniversaries are special moments
   that should be romantically celebrated?

   _____

6. Have you ever cried at a wedding? _____

7. Which is more romantic: a candlelit dinner or a
   picnic in a park? _____

   _____

HOW ROMANTIC ARE YOU?

"You have bewitched me body and soul, and I love, I love, I love you." — Jane Austen, *Pride & Prejudice*

Person B

1. Do you believe in love-at-first sight?

   _____

2. Do you believe in soulmates?

   _____

3. Should a proposal be a planned elaborate moment or quiet and intimate? _____

   _____

4. Do you save cards and letters that you are given?

   _____

   _____

5. True or False: Anniversaries are special moments that should be romantically celebrated?

   _____

6. Have you ever cried at a wedding? _____

7. Which is more romantic: a candlelit dinner or a picnic in a park? _____

   _____

HOW WELL DO YOU KNOW EACH OTHER?

"I have found that if you love life, life will love you back."
— Arthur Rubenstein

Person A

Let's see how much you know about the other person:

1. What is their favorite color? _____

2. What do they typically eat for breakfast?

   _____

3. Would they rather live in the city or the country?

   _____

4. Are they liberal, moderate, or conservative?

   _____

5. What is the first thing they noticed about you?

   _____

6. Would they rather spend an evening home watching a movie or out on the town?

   _____

7. How much time do they spend getting ready in the morning? _____

HOW WELL DO YOU KNOW EACH OTHER?

"Loving you is my greatest strength and my biggest weakness."
— Unknown

Person B

Let's see how much you know about the other person:

1. What is their favorite color? _____

2. What do they typically eat for breakfast?

    _____

3. Would they rather live in the city or the country?

    _____

4. Are they liberal, moderate, or conservative?

    _____

5. What is the first thing they noticed about you?

    _____

6. Would they rather spend an evening home watching a movie or out on the town?

    _____

7. How much time do they spend getting ready in the morning? _____

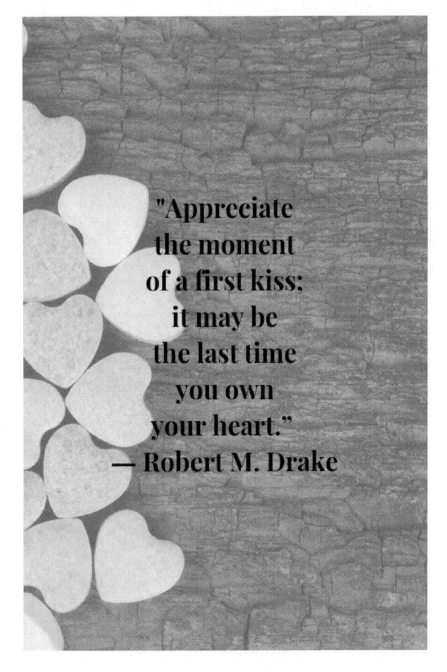

"Appreciate
the moment
of a first kiss;
it may be
the last time
you own
your heart."
— Robert M. Drake

"I don't
ask you
to love me
always like this
but I ask you
to remember,
Somewhere
inside of me
there will always
be the person
I am tonight."
— F. Scott Fitzgerald,
Tender is the Night

MONEY STUFF

"Love's gift cannot be given; it waits to be accepted."
— Rabindranath Tagore

Person A

1. Are prenuptial agreements a good idea, for other people, or an insult? _____

2. Do you have a spending personal budget? _____

   _____

3. If you won $1 million dollars in the lottery, what are two things you would do with the money?

   _____

   _____

4. Do you pay off your credit cards each month?

   _____

5. Do you have any concerns with the way your partner manages their money and spending? _____

   _____

   _____

6. Do you prefer to buy new or used cars? Why? _____

   _____

MONEY STUFF

"Every breath that is in your lungs is a tiny little gift to me."
— The White Stripes, *Dead Leave & The Dirty Ground*

Person B

1. Are prenuptial agreements a good idea, for other people, or an insult? _____

2. Do you have a spending personal budget? _____

   _____

3. If you won $1 million dollars in the lottery, what are two things you would do with the money?

   _____

   _____

4. Do you pay off your credit cards each month?

   _____

5. Do you have any concerns with the way your partner manages their money and spending? _____

   _____

   _____

6. Do you prefer to buy new or used cars? Why? _____

   _____

MONEY STUFF

"For I don't care too much for money, for money can't buy me love." — The Beatles, *Can't Buy Me Love*

Person A

1. What are you currently doing to save for retirement? _____

   _____

2. Is there a major purchase made during the last twelve months that you regret? _____

   _____

3. What percentage of your income do you save each month? _____

   _____

4. What change could you make today that would result in saving an additional $50 a month? _____

   _____

5. What money/financial changes do you want to make? What is stopping you from starting now?

   _____

   _____

   _____

MONEY STUFF

"My philosophy has always been, do what you love and the money will follow." — Amy Weber

Person B

1. What are you currently doing to save for retirement? _____

   _____

2. Is there a major purchase made during the last twelve months that you regret? _____

   _____

3. What percentage of your income do you save each month? _____

   _____

4. What change could you make today that would result in saving an additional $50 a month? _____

   _____

5. What money/financial changes do you want to make? What is stopping you from starting now?

   _____

   _____

   _____

WORK & CAREER

"Appreciate the moment of a first kiss; it may be the last time you own your heart." — Robert M. Drake

Person A

1. When you were a kid, what did you want to be when you grew up? _____

   _____

2. What was your first job? _____

   _____

3. How many jobs have you had during your life? What was your favorite? _____

   _____

4. What was your least favorite job? _____

   _____

5. Would you take a big pay cut to do a job you loved?

   _____

6. Have you ever wanted to own your own business? If yes, what kind of business would it be?

   _____

   _____

WORK & CAREER

"Don't die without embracing the daring adventure your life was meant to be." — Steve Pavlina

Person B

1. When you were a kid, what did you want to be when you grew up? _____

   _____

2. What was your first job? _____

   _____

3. How many jobs have you had during your life? What was your favorite? _____

   _____

4. What was your least favorite job? _____

   _____

5. Would you take a big pay cut to do a job you loved?

   _____

6. Have you ever wanted to own your own business? If yes, what kind of business would it be?

   _____

   _____

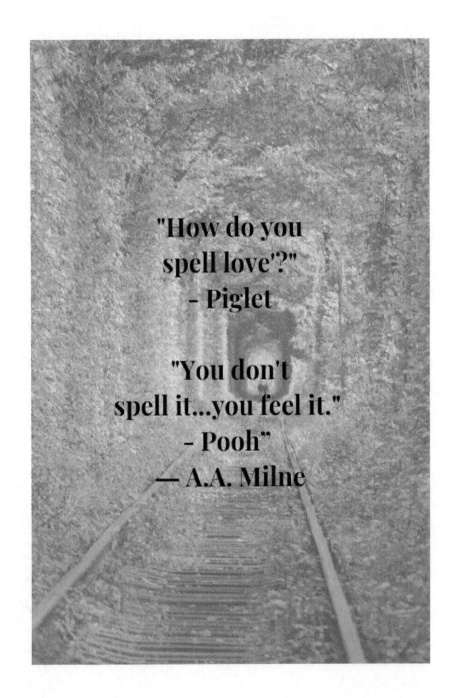

"How do you
spell love'?"
- Piglet

"You don't
spell it...you feel it."
- Pooh"
— A.A. Milne

"If I had
a flower
for every time
I thought
of you
...I could walk
through
my garden
forever."
— Alfred Lord
Tennyson

FOOD

"All you need is love. But a little chocolate now and then doesn't hurt." — Charles Schultz

Person A

1. Would you rather cook or clean-up after?

   _____

2. What is your favorite dessert? _____

   _____

3. Candlelight dinner or breakfast in bed?

   _____

4. What do you like on your pizza? _____

   _____

5. What is your favorite thing to cook? _____

   _____

6. What is your guilty pleasure food? _____

   _____

7. What is your favorite alcoholic drink?

   _____

8. Do you like spicy food? _____

FOOD

"One cannot think well, love well, sleep well, if one has not dined well." — Virginia Woolf, *A Room of One's Own*

Person B

1. Would you rather cook or clean-up after?

    _____

2. What is your favorite dessert? _____

    _____

3. Candlelight dinner or breakfast in bed?

    _____

4. What do you like on your pizza? _____

    _____

5. What is your favorite thing to cook? _____

    _____

6. What is your guilty pleasure food? _____

    _____

7. What is your favorite alcoholic drink?

    _____

9. Do you like spicy food? _____

MORE ON FOOD

"My weaknesses have always been food and men—in that
order." — Dolly Parton

Person A

1. If you could have dinner with any four people who have ever lived, who would you pick?

_____

_____

_____

_____

_____

2. What is your favorite restaurant? _____

_____

3. What is your favorite dish? _____

_____

4. Is there a food item that you refuse to eat?

_____

5. Cake or Pie? _____

6. Favorite cookie? _____

MORE ON FOOD

"There is no love sincerer than the love of food."
— George Bernard Shaw

Person B

1. If you could have dinner with any four people who have ever lived, who would you pick?

_____

_____

_____

_____

_____

2. What is your favorite restaurant? _____

_____

3. What is your favorite dish? _____

_____

4. Is there a food item that you refuse to eat?

_____

5. Cake or Pie? _____

6. Favorite cookie? _____

TRAVEL

"Whatever our souls are made of, his and mine are the same."
— Emily Bronte, *Wuthering Heights*

Person A

1. Do you have a valid passport?

   _____

2. How many countries have you traveled to?

   _____

3. Where would you rather go on vacation: a beach location, camping in the outdoors, to a foreign country, go on a cruise, or a road trip?

   _____

   _____

4. When traveling in another country, do you eat familiar foods or what the locals eat?

   _____

5. Where did you travel on your longest road trip?

   _____

   _____

6. How do you feel about cruises?

   _____

TRAVEL

"Life isn't about finding yourself. Life is about creating yourself." — George Bernard Shaw

Person B

1. Do you have a valid passport?

2. How many countries have you traveled to?

3. Where would you rather go on vacation: a beach location, camping in the outdoors, to a foreign country, go on a cruise, or a road trip?

4. When traveling in another country, do you eat familiar foods or what the locals eat?

5. Where did you travel on your longest road trip?

6. How do you feel about cruises?

TRAVEL BUCKET LIST

"Some people come in our life as blessings. Some come in your life as lessons." — Mother Teresa

Person A

List the top 10 places you would visit if money and time were no concern.

1. _____

2. _____

3. _____

4. _____

5. _____

6. _____

7. _____

8. _____

9. _____

10. _____

TRAVEL BUCKET LIST

"True forgiveness is when you can say, "Thank you for that experience." — Oprah Winfrey

Person B

List the top 10 places you would visit if money and time were no concern.

1. _____

2. _____

3. _____

4. _____

5. _____

6. _____

7. _____

8. _____

9. _____

10. _____

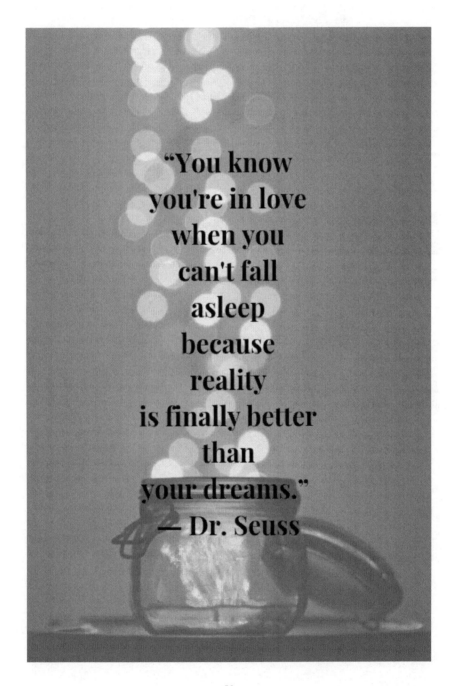

"You know you're in love when you can't fall asleep because reality is finally better than your dreams." — Dr. Seuss

"But
most of all
I'm afraid
of walking
out that door
and never
feeling again
for my
whole life
the way I feel
when I'm
with you"
— Baby, Dirty Dancing

SPIRITUALITY & RELIGION

"You only have to forgive once. To resent, you have to do it all day, every day."
— M.L. Stedman

Person A

1. Were your parents religious when you were a kid?

    _____

    _____

2. Do you have a current religious or spiritual practice
    that is important to you? What is it? _____

    _____

    _____

3. Do you pray? If yes, how often? _____

    _____

4. What do you think is the purpose of life?

    _____

    _____

5. Which do you think has the most impact on our
    lives: fate or free will? _____

    _____

SPIRITUALITY & RELIGION

"Never love anyone who treats you like you're ordinary."
— Oscar Wilde

Person B

1. Were your parents religious when you were a kid?

   _____

   _____

2. Do you have a current religious or spiritual practice
   that is important to you? What is it? _____

   _____

   _____

3. Do you pray? If yes, how often? _____

   _____

4. What do you think is the purpose of life?

   _____

   _____

5. Which do you think has the most impact on our
   lives: fate or free will? _____

   _____

QUESTIONS

"Lovers don't finally meet somewhere.
They're in each other all along." — Rumi

Person A

1. What is the accomplishment you are most proud of?

   _____

   _____

   _____

2. Were you ever in a relationship with someone your
   parents didn't like? _____

   _____

3. Do you often need alone time? If yes, how will you
   let me know? _____

   _____

   _____

4. Is there a quote you live by? _____

   _____

   _____

5. What is your greatest fear? _____

   _____

QUESTIONS

"The greatest thing you'll ever learn Is to love and be loved in return." — Natalie Cole

Person B

1. What is the accomplishment you are most proud of?

   _____

   _____

   _____

2. Were you ever in a relationship with someone your parents didn't like? _____

   _____

3. Do you often need alone time? If yes, how will you let me know? _____

   _____

   _____

4. Is there a quote you live by? _____

   _____

   _____

5. What is your greatest fear? _____

   _____

POLITICAL STUFF

"When love is not madness it is not love."
— Pedro Calderón de la Barca

Person A

1. Who was the best president of your lifetime?

   _____

2. Is there an issue that you would publicly protest
   for? Have you ever participated in a march or
   boycott? _____

   _____

   _____

3. What do you think are the three most serious issues
   facing the world today? _____

   _____

   _____

   _____

4. When was the last time you voted?

   _____

5. Have you ever donated your time or money to a
   political candidate? _____

   _____

POLITICAL STUFF

"Anyone can love a rose, but it takes a lot to love a thorn."
— Tom Flynn

Person B

1. Who was the best president of your lifetime?

   _____

2. Is there an issue that you would publicly protest
   for? Have you ever participated in a march or
   boycott? _____

   _____

   _____

3. What do you think are the three most serious issues
   facing the world today? _____

   _____

   _____

   _____

4. When was the last time you voted?

   _____

5. Have you ever donated your time or money to a
   political candidate? _____

   _____

WHAT DO YOU WANT FROM LIFE?

"You're the reason I am breathing, yet you often take my breath away" — Unknown

Person A

Mark each statement with: Definitely, Maybe, or No

1. I want to be famous: _____

2. I want a career that is focused on helping others.

   _____

3. I want a career that is focused on making money.

   _____

4. I want people to like me. _____

5. I want my family to be proud of me. _____

6. I want to be important. _____

7. It is okay to often sacrifice personal time for career goals. _____

8. I want people to think I am physically attractive.

   _____

9. I want to change my community:

   _____

WHAT DO YOU WANT FROM LIFE?

"All, everything I understand, I only understand because I love." — Leo Tolstoy, *War and Peace*

Person B

Mark each statement with: Definitely, Maybe, or No

1. I want to be famous: _____

2. I want a career that is focused on helping others.

   _____

3. I want a career that is focused on making money.

   _____

4. I want people to like me. _____

5. I want my family to be proud of me. _____

6. I want to be important. _____

7. It is okay to often sacrifice personal time for career goals. _____

8. I want people to think I am physically attractive.

   _____

9. I want to change my community:

   _____

"Being
deeply
loved
by someone
gives you strength,
while
loving
someone deeply
gives you
courage."
— Laozi

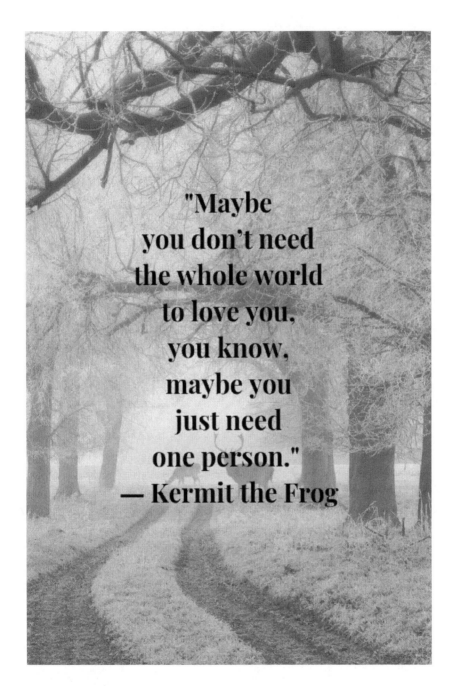

"Maybe
you don't need
the whole world
to love you,
you know,
maybe you
just need
one person."
— Kermit the Frog

ABOUT YOU

"Love is just a word until someone comes along and gives it meaning" — Paulo Coelho

Person A

1. What would be a good title for your autobiography?

   _____

   _____

2. Do you think you could still pass the written portion of the driver's test without studying?

   _____

3. What is your favorite line from a movie?

   _____

   _____

4. Do you believe in life on other planets?

   _____

5. What is your favorite color? _____

6. If you were forced to sing karaoke, what song would you pick to perform?

   _____

   _____

7. What was your first pet? What was its name?

   _____

   _____

ABOUT YOU

"The heart has a heart of its own,"
— Morrissey, *It's Not Your Birthday Anymore*

Person B

1. What would be a good title for your autobiography?

   _____

   _____

2. Do you think you could still pass the written portion of the driver's test without studying?

   _____

3. What is your favorite line from a movie?

   _____

   _____

4. Do you believe in life on other planets?

   _____

5. What is your favorite color? _____

6. If you were forced to sing karaoke, what song would you pick to perform?

   _____

   _____

7. What was your first pet? What was its name?

   _____

   _____

THIS IS ME

"True love is rare, and it's the only thing that gives life real meaning." — Nicholas Sparks, *Message in a Bottle*

Person A

1. When you were a kid, did you ever dream about becoming a professional athlete? Which sport?

   _____

2. What was your favorite candy when you were a kid?

   _____

3. Have you ever broken a bone?

   _____

4. Name a movie you could watch over and over.

   _____

   _____

5. Rollercoasters: Yes or No? _____

6. Are psychics real or a scam? _____

7. What is your least favorite household chore?

   _____

8. What was your SAT/ACT score? _____

   _____

THIS IS ME

"It's like in that moment the whole universe existed just to bring us together" — Maddie Eckels, Serendipity

Person B

1. When you were a kid, did you ever dream about becoming a professional athlete? Which sport?

   _____

2. What was your favorite candy when you were a kid?

   _____

3. Have you ever broken a bone?

   _____

4. Name a movie you could watch over and over.

   _____

   _____

5. Rollercoasters: Yes or No? _____

6. Are psychics real or a scam? _____

7. What is your least favorite household chore?

   _____

8. What was your SAT/ACT score? _____

   _____

GOOD TO KNOW

"You don't take away my choices. You are my choice."
— Colleen Houck

Person A

1. When an uncomfortable situation occurs, do you usually confront or avoid it? _____

2. Would you be willing to move to enhance your partner's career? _____

3. What are your thoughts on being a parent?

    _____

    _____

    _____

4. What is your biggest regret from a past relationship? _____

    _____

    _____

    _____

5. What is the dollar amount one person in a relationship should spend up to without having to consult the other person? _____

    _____

GOOD TO KNOW

"People call those imperfections, but no, that's the good stuff."
— Johah Howells, *Good Will Hunting*

Person B

1. When an uncomfortable situation occurs, do you usually confront or avoid it? _____

2. Would you be willing to move to enhance your partner's career? _____

3. What are your thoughts on being a parent?

   _____

   _____

   _____

4. What is your biggest regret from a past relationship? _____

   _____

   _____

   _____

5. What is the dollar amount one person in a relationship should spend up to without having to consult the other person? _____

   _____

BUCKET LIST

"Romance is the glamour which turns the dust of everyday life into a golden haze." — Elinor Glyn

Person A

List the top 10 things you want to accomplish or experience during your life.

1. _____

2. _____

3. _____

4. _____

5. _____

6. _____

7. _____

8. _____

9. _____

10. _____

BUCKET LIST

So, I love you because the entire universe conspired
to help me find you." — Paulo Coelho, The Alchemist

Person B

List the top 10 things you want to accomplish or experience during your life.

1. _____

2. _____

3. _____

4. _____

5. _____

6. _____

7. _____

8. _____

9. _____

10. _____

"In all
the world,
there is
no heart
for me
like yours.
In all the world,
there is no love
for you
like mine."
— Maya
Angelou

"Love is a fire.
But whether
it is going
to warm
your hearth
or burn down
your house,
you can
never tell."
— Joan Crawford

JUST CURIOUS

"We love because it is the only true adventure."
— Nikki Giovanni

Person A

1. If you could only pick one, would you choose to be in love or to be rich? _____

   _____

2. What is your favorite thing about yourself?

   _____

   _____

3. Do you remember your dreams? _____

   _____

4. What is the best pick-up line you have ever used or heard? _____

   _____

   _____

5. Valentine's Day: Important or Trivial?

   _____

6. Do you have a library card?

   _____

JUST CURIOUS

"Love is friendship set on fire."
— Jeremy Taylor

Person B

7. If you could only pick one, would you choose to be in love or to be rich? _____

_____

8. What is your favorite thing about yourself?

_____

_____

9. Do you remember your dreams? _____

_____

10. What is the best pick-up line you have ever used or heard? _____

_____

_____

11. Valentine's Day: Important or Trivial?

_____

12. Do you have a library card?

_____

TRIVIA

"It is not a lack of love, but a lack of friendship that makes an unhappy marriage" — Friedrich Nietzsche

Person A

1. Are you a dog or cat person?

   _____

2. Do you have any allergies?

   _____

3. Have you ever collected anything during your life?

   _____

4. Did you go to summer camp as a kid?

   _____

5. High school reunions: (A.) "I can't wait," (B) "We will see when the time arrives," or (C) "Do people do that?" _____

   _____

6. What is your favorite salad dressing?

   _____

7. Do you know how to change a tire?

   _____

TRIVIA

"They may forget what you said, but they will never forget how you made them feel." — Carl W. Buechner

Person B

1. Are you a dog or cat person?

   _____

2. Do you have any allergies?

   _____

3. Have you ever collected anything during your life?

   _____

4. Did you go to summer camp as a kid?

   _____

5. High school reunions: (A.) "I can't wait," (B) "We will see when the time arrives," or (C) "Do people do that?" _____

   _____

6. What is your favorite salad dressing?

   _____

7. Do you know how to change a tire?

   _____

Where Will You Be?

"No road is long with good company."
—Turkish Proverb

Person A

Where do you see yourself in five years in the following areas?

- Personal Life: _____

  _____

- Career: _____

  _____

- Finances: _____

  _____

Ten years?

- Personal Life: _____

  _____

- Career: _____

  _____

- Finances: _____

  _____

Where Will You Be?

"Beauty is not in the face; beauty is a light in the heart."
—Khalil Gibran

Person B

Where do you see yourself in five years in the following areas?

- Personal Life: _____

  _____

- Career: _____

  _____

- Finances: _____

  _____

Ten years?

- Personal Life: _____

  _____

- Career: _____

  _____

- Finances: _____

  _____

PERSONAL FINANCE

"Too many people spend money to buy things they don't want to impress people that they don't like." — Will Rogers

Person A

It is important to understand each other's spending and saving tendencies. The following multiple-choice questions will assist the two of you to understand where you are alike and differ, while also showing where the two of you need to communicate and focus.

1. My primary feelings about money are:
   - Anxiety. There is never enough.
   - Satisfaction. It's a way to get things I want.
   - Safety. Money is security.
   - Happiness. I have more than enough for the basics.
2. My main money goal is:
   - To be able to afford the basics.
   - To earn enough to spend on things that I want.
   - To save for retirement.
3. If I came into a large sum of money, I would:
   - Pay down my debt.
   - Save or invest it
   - Give it to charity
   - Purchase items from my want list.
4. My relationship with money is:
   - I am very focused on making more.
   - It is a stress point for me, and I avoid dealing with it.
   - I am very frugal and am more focused on saving.
   - It is a source of happiness, comfort, and prestige.

PERSONAL FINANCE

"Opportunity is missed by most people because it is dressed in overalls and looks like work." — Thomas Edison

Still Person A

5. My money budgeting habits are:
   - Focused. I have a structured budget that I adhere to.
   - Scattered. I try to budget but am often not successful.
   - Nonexistent. I don't have a good idea on how much I spend, and I don't save or invest anything.

6. My opinions on credit cards are:
   - I have several and carry a balance forward each month.
   - I rarely use them and always pay them off when I do.
   - I prefer to use cash or my debit card.

7. When I want to buy something that is outside my budget, I:
   - Borrow money or use a credit card.
   - Use my savings.
   - Save up enough to purchase it.
   - I don't have a budget.

8. How do you handle an unexpected financial emergency?
   - I am unsure how I would afford an unexpected expense.
   - I would have to take out a loan or use a credit card.
   - I have money set aside for emergencies.
   - In the last year I have had to use a high interest loan or a payday loan to take care of an emergency.

9. My spending habits are:
   - I enjoy buying things and spend on things I want.
   - I am very careful and tend to only spend on the basics.
   - I stick to a budget but allow room for the occasional splurge.
   - Spending money makes me nervous so I avoid it.
   - I make money and I spend money.

PERSONAL FINANCE

"It is not the man who has too little, but the man who craves more, that is poor." — Seneca

Person B

It is important to understand each other's spending and saving tendencies. The following multiple-choice questions will assist the two of you to understand where you are alike and differ, while also showing where the two of you need to communicate and focus.

1. My primary feelings about money are:
    - Anxiety. There is never enough.
    - Satisfaction. It's a way to get things I want.
    - Safety. Money is security.
    - Happiness. I have more than enough for the basics.
2. My main money goal is:
    - To be able to afford the basics.
    - To earn enough to spend on things that I want.
    - To save for retirement.
3. If I came into a large sum of money, I would:
    - Pay down my debt.
    - Save or invest it
    - Give it to charity
    - Purchase items from my want list.
4. My relationship with money is:
    - I am very focused on making more.
    - It is a stress point for me, and I avoid dealing with it.
    - I am very frugal and am more focused on saving.
    - It is a source of happiness, comfort, and prestige.

PERSONAL FINANCE

"Empty pockets never held anyone back. Only empty heads and empty hearts can do that." — Norman Vincent Peale

Still Person B

5. My money budgeting habits are:
    - Focused. I have a structured budget that I adhere to.
    - Scattered. I try to budget but am often not successful.
    - Nonexistent. I don't have a good idea on how much I spend, and I don't save or invest anything.
6. My opinions on credit cards are:
    - I have several and carry a balance forward each month.
    - I rarely use them and always pay them off when I do.
    - I prefer to use cash or my debit card.
7. When I want to buy something that is outside my budget, I:
    - Borrow money or use a credit card.
    - Use my savings.
    - Save up enough to purchase it.
    - I don't have a budget.
8. How do you handle an unexpected financial emergency?
    - I am unsure how I would afford an unexpected expense.
    - I would have to take out a loan or use a credit card.
    - I have money set aside for emergencies.
    - In the last year I have had to use a high interest loan or a payday loan to take care of an emergency.
9. My spending habits are:
    - I enjoy buying things and spend on things I want.
    - I am very careful and tend to only spend on the basics.
    - I stick to a budget but allow room for the occasional splurge.
    - Spending money makes me nervous so I avoid it.
    - I make money and I spend money.

"We
stumbled
on a view
that's
tailor-made
for two."
— Andrea Brusig
La La Land

"And in the end,
we were
all just humans,
drunk on
the idea
that love,
only love,
could heal
our brokenness"
— F. Scott Fitzgerald
The Great Gatsby

MOVIES, MUSIC, & BOOKS

"Don't it always seem to go, that you don't know what you've got till it's gone." — Joni Mitchell, *Big Yellow Taxi*

Person A

1. Is there a book you have read more than once?

   _____

2. What is the last thing you binge-watched?

   _____

3. If you could be a character in any movie, past or present, which one would you pick? _____

   _____

4. What is the last movie you saw that you loved?

   _____

5. What is your favorite genre of music?

   _____

6. What was the first concert you went to?

   _____

7. What is the best concert you have attended?

   _____

MOVIES, MUSIC, & BOOKS

"Nothing is impossible, the word itself says 'I'm possible'!"
— Audrey Hepburn

Person B

1. Is there a book you have read more than once?

   _____

2. What is the last thing you binge-watched?

   _____

3. If you could be a character in any movie, past or present, which one would you pick? _____

   _____

4. What is the last movie you saw that you loved?

   _____

5. What is your favorite genre of music?

   _____

6. What was the first concert you went to?

   _____

7. What is the best concert you have attended?

   _____

TOP TEN MOVIES

"Here's looking at you kid."
—Rick Blaine, *Casablanca*

Person A

List Your Top Ten Favorite Movies:

1. _____

2. _____

3. _____

4. _____

5. _____

6. _____

7. _____

8. _____

9. _____

10. _____

TOP TEN MOVIES

"You had me at hello."
— Dorothy Boyd, *Jerry McGuire*

Person B

List Your Top Ten Favorite Movies:

1. _____

2. _____

3. _____

4. _____

5. _____

6. _____

7. _____

8. _____

9. _____

10. _____

TOP TEN SONGS

"And suddenly you're all I need, the reason why I smile."
— Avril Lavigne, *Smile*

Person A

List Your Top Ten Favorite Songs:

1. _____

2. _____

3. _____

4. _____

5. _____

6. _____

7. _____

8. _____

9. _____

10. _____

TOP TEN SONGS

"Before the day I met you, life was so unkind. But you're the key to my peace of mind." — Aretha Franklin, *A Natural Woman*

Person B

List Your Top Ten Favorite Songs:

1. _____

2. _____

3. _____

4. _____

5. _____

6. _____

7. _____

8. _____

9. _____

10. _____

MOVIES ABOUT COUPLES

"I miss you Jenny. If there is anything you need, I won't be far away." — Forest Gump, *Forest Gump*

- Top Hat (1935)
- Camille (1936)
- My Little Chickadee (1940)
- Casablanca (1942)
- Woman of the Year (1942)
- An Affair to Remember (1945)
- It's a Wonderful Life (1946)
- Roman Holiday (1953)
- To Catch a Thief (1955)
- Breakfast at Tiffany's (1961)
- Westside Story (1961)
- Cleopatra (1963)
- Love Story (1970)
- The Way We Were (1973)
- Rocky (1976)
- Grease (1978)
- Superman (1978)
- Valley Girl (1983)
- Swing Shift (1984)
- Sixteen Candles (1984)
- Out of Africa (1985)

MOVIES ABOUT COUPLES

"You want the moon? Just say the word, and I'll throw a lasso around it and pull it down." —George Baily, *It's a Wonderful Life*

- Dirty Dancing (1987)
- The Princess Bride (1987)
- Moonstruck (1987)
- Bull Durham (1988)
- When Harry Met Sally (1989)
- Say Anything (1998)
- Pretty Woman (1990)
- Ghost (1990)
- My Girl (1991)
- Sleepless in Seattle (1993)
- Forest Gump (1994)
- Before Sunrise (1995)
- The Bridges of Madison County (1995)
- Jerry McGuire (1996)
- Romeo + Juliet (1996)
- The English Patient (1996)
- Titanic (1997)
- As Good As It Gets (1997)
- Fools Rush In (1997)
- Good Will Hunting (1997)
- Shakespeare in Love (1998)

MORE MOVIES ABOUT COUPLES

"I love you. You complete me."
— Jerry McGuire, *Jerry McGuire*

- Hope Floats (1998)
- You've Got Mail (1998)
- How Stella Got Her Groove Back (1998)
- Meet Joe Black (1998)
- 10 Things I Hate About You (1999)
- Notting Hill (1999)
- Love and Basketball (2000)
- Save the Last Dance (2001)
- Bridget Jones's Diary (2001)
- Serendipity (2001)
- Moulin Rouge (2001)
- Sweet Home Alabama (2002)
- My Big Fat Greek Wedding (2002)
- Something's Gotta Give (2003)
- Big Fish (2003)
- How to Lose a Guy in 10 Days (2003)
- Love Actually (2003)
- Eternal Sunshine of the Spotless Mind (2004)
- The Notebook (2004)
- 50 First Dates (2004)
- Incredibles (2004)

MORE MOVIES ABOUT COUPLES

"I'm also just a girl, standing in front of a boy, asking him to love her." — Anna Scott, Notting Hill

- Brokeback Mountain (2005)
- Pride and Prejudice (2005)
- Slumdog Millionaire (2005)
- High School Musical (2006)
- Juno (2007)
- Sex in the City: The Movie (2008)
- Twilight (2008)
- 500 Hundred Days of Summer (2009)
- It's Complicated (2009)
- Date Night (2010)
- Crazy, Stupid, Love (2011)
- The Vow (2012)
- Silver Linings Playbook (2012)
- The Perks of Being a Wallflower (2012)
- The Fault in Our Stars (2012)
- The Hunger Games (2012)
- Great Expectations (2013)
- Blue is the Warmest Color (2013)
- La La Land (2016)
- Southside With You (2016)
- Incredibles 2 (2018)

RELATIONSHIP PLAYLIST

"We're still having fun and you're still the one." — Orleans, *Still the One*

- "All My Love" by Patti Page (1950)
- "Because of You" by Tony Bennett (1951)
- "I'm Yours" by Eddie Fisher (1952)
- "No Other Love" by Perry Como (1953)
- "Earth Angel" by The Penguins (1954)
- "Only You and You Alone" by The Platters (1955)
- "I Walk the Line" by Johnny Cash (1956)
- "When I Fall in Love" by Nat King Cole (1956)
- "Everyday" by Buddy Holly (1957)
- "To Be Loved" by Jackie Wilson (1958)
- I Only Have Eyes for You" by The Flamingos (1959)
- "At Last" by Etta James (1960)
- "Can't Help Falling In Love by Elvis Presley (1961)
- "Soldier Boy" by The Shirelles (1962)
- "So Much In Love" by The Tymes (1963)
- "My Guy" by Mary Wells (1964)
- "The Way You Look Tonight" by Frank Sinatra (1965)
- "I Got You Babe" by Sonny & Cher (1965)
- "In My Life" By The Beatles (1965)
- "God Only Knows" by The Beach Boys (1966)
- "(Your Love Keeps Lifting Me) Higher and Higher" by Jackie Wilson (1967)
- "When I'm Sixty-Four by The Beatles (1967)
- "You're All I Need to Get By" by Marvin Gaye and Tammi Terrell (1968)
- "Sweet Caroline" by Neil Diamond (1969)

RELATIONSHIP PLAYLIST

"Love is Never Wrong."
— Melissa Ethridge*e*

- "I'll Be There" by The Jackson 5 (1970)
- "I Feel the Earth Move" by Carole King (1971)
- "Your Song" by Elton John (1971)
- "An Old-Fashioned Love Song" by Three Dog Night (1971)
- "Let's Say Together" by Al Green (1972)
- "Loves Me Like a Rock" by Paul Simon (1973)
- "Lovin' You" by Minnie Riperton (1974)
- "I Will Always Love You" by Dolly Parton (1974)
- "This Will Be an Everlasting Love" by Natalie Cole (1975)
- "Love Will Keep Us Together" by Captain & Tenille (1975)
- "Still the One" by Orleans (1976)
- "How Deep is Your Love" by Bee Gees (1977)
- "Just the Way You Are" by Billy Joel (1977)
- "Count on Me" by Jefferson Starship (1978)
- "You Decorated My Life" by Kenny Rogers (1979)
- "Keep on Loving You" by REO Speedwagon (1980)
- "Through the Years" by Kenny Rogers (1981)
- "Don't Stop Believin'" by Journey (1981)
- "I Melt With You" by Modern English (1982)
- "Whatever Happened to Old Fashioned Love" by B.J. Thomas (1983)
- "You're the Inspiration" by Chicago (1984)
- "Time After Time" by Cyndi Lauper (1984)
- "You Give Good Love" Whitney Houston (1985)

RELATIONSHIP PLAYLIST

"And, in the end the love you take is equal to the love you make." — Paul McCartney, *The End*

- "Love Will Conquer All" by Lionel Richie (1986)
- "Together Forever" by Rick Astley (1987)
- "Strong Enough to Bend", Tanya Tucker (1988)
- "Where've You Been" by Kathy Madea (1989)
- "Lovesong" by The Cure (1989)
- "I'd Love You All Over Again" by Alan Jackson (1990)
- "Unfinished Symphony" by Massive Attack (1991)
- "Harvest Moon" by Neil Young (1992)
- "In This Life" by Collin Raye (1992)
- "Have I Told You Lately That I Love You?" By Rod Stewart (1993)
- "Anniversary" by Cowboy Junkies (1993)
- "I'll Stand by You" by The Pretenders (1994)
- "One Boy, One Girl" by Collin Raye (1995)
- "I'm Still in Love With You" by New Edition (1996)
- "Truly Madly Deeply "by Savage Garden (1997)
- "You're Still the One" by Shania Twain (1998)
- "In Spite of Ourselves" by John Prine & Iris DeMent (1999)
- "Amazed" by Lonestar (1999)
- "Grow Old With Me" by Mary Chapin Carpenter (1999)
- "Power of Two" by The Indigo Girls (2000)
- "The Luckiest" by Ben Folds (2001)
- "I Wanna Grow Old With You by Westlife (2001)
- "Come Away With Me" by Norah Jones (2002)

RELATIONSHIP PLAYLIST
"...because being with you makes perfect sense"
— Tim McGraw

- "This is the Good Stuff" by Kenny Chesney (2002)
- "Crazy in Love" by Beyoncé (2003)
- "Remember When" by Alan Jackson (2003)
- "Stay With You" by John Legend (2004)
- "Sometimes You Can't Make It on Your Own" by U2 (2004)
- "Do You Remember" by Jack Johnson (2005)
- "I'll Follow You Into the Dark" by Death Cab For Cutie (2005)
- We Belong Together by Mariah Carey (2005)
- "My Love" by Justin Timberlake (2006)
- "Whatever it Takes" by Lifehouse (2007)
- "The Story" by Brandi Carlisle (2007)
- "Still Feels Good" by Rascal Flatts (2007)
- "Love Story" by Taylor Swift (2008)
- "Never Say Never" by The Fray (2009)
- "Just the Way You Are" by Bruno Mars (2010)
- "Stuck Like Glue" by Sugarland (2010)
- "Love on Top" by Beyoncé (2011)
- "I Won't Give Up" by Jason Mraz (2012)
- "Just Give Me a Reason" by P!NK and Nate Ruess (2012)
- "Still Into You" by Paramore (2013)
- "Thinking Out Loud" by Ed Sheeran (2014)
- "Remedy" by Adele (2015)
- "Grow Old" by Florida Georgia Line (2016)
- "Perfect" by Ed Sheeran (2017)
- "Love" by Kendrick Lamar (2017)
- "Good as You" by Kane Brown (2018)

AVAILABLE ON AMAZON!

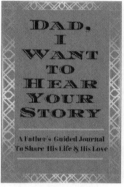

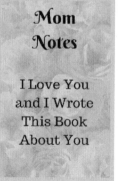

THIS BOOK

Couples who are truly close and resilient don't just happen; they become that way by trusting one another, leaning on each other, and learning from each other.

This book was written with the goal of giving couples a fun way to learn about each other and to share their individual experiences. If you enjoy this book, a review on Amazon would be helpful in helping others find it. Thank you and I am more than honored that you picked this book to spend time with.

I also have several other books focused on guiding people to tell their stories and share their life.

- Mom, I Want to Hear Your Story

- Dad, I Want to Hear Your Story

- Grandmother, I Want to Hear Your Story: A Grandmother's Guided Journal to Share Her Life and Her Love

- Grandfather, I Want to Hear Your Story: A Grandfather's Guided Journal to Share His Life and His Love

- Because I Love You: The Couple's Bucket List That Builds Your Relationship

- Mom Notes: I Wrote This Book About the Best Mother Ever

- Love Notes: I Wrote This Book About You

- Dad Notes: Dad, I Wrote This Book for You

ABOUT THE AUTHOR

Jeffrey Mason has devoted his professional life to helping individuals, couples, and organizations achieve goals and create positive impacts.

He is committed to the idea that the more we do for each other, the more we do for ourselves and the world.

If you get a chance, checkout and "like" his Facebook author page at www.facebook.com/JeffreyMasonAuthor and leave a review for this book on Amazon. Your feedback helps him get better at this thing he loves.

You can also contact him at hello@jeffreymason.com and his books can be found at:

- www.amazon.com/author/jeffreymason

- www.amazon.com/author/eyppublishing

You can also reach him at:

- www.jeffreymason.com

- www.facebook.com/JeffreyMasonAuthor

He would love to hear from you.

"We're all
a little weird.
And life is a little weird.
And when we
find someone
whose weirdness
is compatible
with ours,
we join up with them
and fall into
mutually satisfying
weirdness
and call it love,
true love."
— Robert Fulghum,
True Love

"I vow
to fiercely
love you
in all your forms,
now and forever.
I promise
to never forget
that this is
a once
in a lifetime love."
— Leo,
The Vow

Made in the USA
Middletown, DE
30 May 2024

55072432R00057